New Poets Seven features both youth and maturity; three
different voices orchestrated to produce an engaging harmony
of life. Carefully chosen from many manuscripts, once again
South Australian poets have demonstrated that they can take
their place with the nation's best.

David Cookson
CONVENOR,
FRIENDLY STREET POETS

FRIENDLY STREET
new poets seven

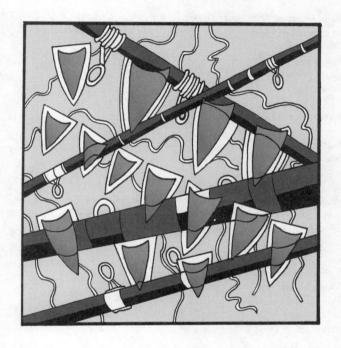

Travelling with Bligh Kate Deller-Evans

Night Fishing Jim Puckridge

Triangular Light Melanie Duckworth

Friendly Street Poets

Wakefield
Press

Friendly Street Poets Incorporated
in association with
Wakefield Press
Box 2266
Kent Town
South Australia 5071

First Published 2002

Cover illustration by Jonathon Inverarity
Designed and typeset by Gina Inverarity
Printed and bound by Hyde Park Press, Adelaide

ISBN 186254 567 7

Government
of South Australia

A R T S A

Friendly Street is supported by the
South Australian Government
through Arts SA.

CONTENTS

TRAVELLING WITH BLIGH

by **Kate Deller-Evans**

Kate Deller-Evans is a lecturer in academic
writing and study skills at Flinders University.
She grew up in North Adelaide and Fitzroy
and holidayed in the miner's cottage her
mother bought on the Yorke Peninsula.
She is married to Steve Evans — theirs is a
household brimming with children where they
enjoy reading, writing and deep discussion.

ACKNOWLEDGEMENTS

Versions of some poems have appeared in:
Alive the Spirit; *Elledit*; *Fluorescent Voices*;
Friendly Street 22; *Gawler Bunyip*; *Ripples on
the Water*; *Sleeping Under a Grand Piano*;
The Colonial Athens; *University Readings 3*;
and have been heard on Radio 5UV

When we were postgrad education students at
Adelaide Stephen Lawrence signed me up for
a writing class organised by Robert Brown.
Peter McFarlane and subsequently Jeff Guess
were fine workshop teachers there. I have been
fortunate to encounter other poets willing to
share their expertise, particularly Kevin
Roberts and most recently Jan Owen in
Jeri Kroll's course at Flinders. Listening to
contemporary poets is essential and I
commend Friendly Street for its forum and
Geoff Page in Canberra for his marvellous
series of readings at Chats. Belonging to a
group of writers has been helpful; thank you
A Passion of Poets. Lorrie, Matthew, and John,
what good times we had at Moonta.

In memory of SMD.

Steve: you bring me all this.

THE POEMS

The Barman and Bligh

the harbour is out of sight
down here the dank sandstone's
rum soaked, barrel-bound

together we are holed in
this basement internment
a switch: the leaders now the led

of course the men were unhappy
along the length of the bar
they've swilled their discontent

but to have predicted this?
a prisoner in my own hotel, beyond
the shimmery dust, the sweat of roadside teams

Bligh's bluster's evaporated
his choleric cheeks are pale
as washed flagstones

the troopers have dropped their eyes
as if by meeting his gaze they assent
caught by default: by choice they'd be captors

his silence is a new fear in such damp
where rule of clanking iron has landed us
in this shrine to settlement

Sailing the Heaps

Whole villages migrated
to mine a better life
in exodus a journey
to drought-ridden land,
a Cornwall of the south.

As children we holidayed
the coastal town
cast eyes from crow's-nest
atop the slag heaps
with parkas raised above our heads
as coloured spinnakers
we'd fly the cementation runnels
delight in the wild space
acrid air, weird earth.

When the copper was gone
the landscape was barren
without fresh water
disease had swept them off
unchartered on the district museum model
a terrible herringbone pattern
rows of little mounds
the unmarked graves of children.

Slag Heaps

It was the discovery
to revive the state

drew miners across the border
and from Cornish villages

veins rich with promised ore
deep under the flesh of hard rock.

Now, on the road to Moonta
the last corner from Kadina

unveils the devastation
the skin of the land

carbuncled with mesa boils
red sores of waste

the inadequate process of dirt
a cover-up with copper powder.

93 Moonta Rd., North Yelta

on the smooth pine table
scrubbed new with sandsoap

each morning at ten
breakfast as a performance

in one large electric pan
Mum fried: eggs, tomatoes, bacon

we all watched the preparation
our own participation, half the fun

on the toaster from the antique mart
we took turns burning our fingers

drawing the stainless steel flap
fiddling the bread to twist it

brown the other side —
they were slow starts to the day

even now if ever I cook
the full breakfast

I smell holidays

coppery, salty-hot air
through early morning mist

Under the Planks

Moonta Bay

until the line of weed
water lucid as green jelly

surface warmth
depth cold

above, towels laid out
jetty-dry under sun

and me, aged nine
skimming below

daring into the sea-ink
following glitter of lights

a fleetingly world
shoal of fish

Sick Feet

over my bed's rail
poking from pjs
my bare feet
I'm sick, confined
and bored

reach for sketchbook
dash strokes of ink

they are long feet
long toes, worm toes
the second digit long
as my thumb
and bony
the bump on top
high enough
if tightly laced
schoolshoes rub
leave bruises

this spider scrawl
counts as homework
life drawing: self-portrait
sick in bed with sick feet
nails scraping over the brass

Twin

hitched under armpits
mine the left, the vanilla nipple
yours premium, chocolate
the way it goes
splitting tasks, doubling the pain
at school you excelled while
I hopped desks, swotted flies
like our cat pawing at tadpoles
we'd caught in the creek
with jam tins, no string
hoping to grow frogs
slip them down Evelyn's shirt
of all the girls hers
the first breasts to swell
to burst into high school

we would repeat it — that obsession
wanting always the same girl
night after night I dreamt
punches to your face
exercising my swift will
against your calm handsome
I never told you how at university
on that orientation camp at the beach
your first real love
crawled into my bunk
it was delicious
like our mother's milk

which I can taste
at the corner of my mouth
its cream globule
ready for my tongue
though under my suit
my knees feel raw
as if the blood
that first clotted there
the day you shoved me
to the gravel path
still itches

My Father as Puck

I see him best
through his own story
1949, a university lark
when Sydney City Council
was demolishing men's loos
all over town, George Street ones
the prosh students
thought worth saving
of architectural merit
razed in the name of progress.

The lads dressed in drag
as fairies
wings, wands, tutus and all
spun a maypole dance
round the toilet block
threading ribbons
as they twirled.

When the police pounced
my dad was one of a few
to jump the ramshackle truck
a mature-aged student
had the foresight to bring.

Back on campus
the lanky Pucks
wrought wicked magic

took their finery
to the Girls Only Refectory
lined up with their trays
for their luncheon.

They were pursued
but I can see them
hear them still
in the arched quadrangle
flitting by with their
just deep voices
helloing to a later world.

Heritage Wall, 1988

Ovingham

The eastern boundary capped
in a frill of broken bottles
once the length of the suburb
divided rich on the hill
from the poor below
a colony of managers,
factory bosses.
Self-made men.

Our villa one such — builder built
at the start of the century.
The wall: older. And over it
in the paddock
dray horses
ploughing no trade
but munching the green,
content.

Under cover of a working day
the demolition.
New cement render
for the little boxes —
homes for the elderly,
infirm, lonely.

Planted in my black soil
the shards of broken glass.

Through the kitchen window

the laden plum tree
baubles which will drop
all at once
three days before Christmas
while we are away
ripe, purple, they will rot
and we won't scoop this
bounteous harvest
but for compost

our garden filled with trees
produce for each season
figs for jam
juice from the orange
lemon on pancakes
twinned apple boughs
festive green and red
gathered in succession
nectarines, scarce in shops
fresh, dripping
over my bare flesh
arms reaching to pluck
from branches: higher, higher

from the window in the house
I never owned with you
fruit we never cherished

Painting Hamlet

I am doing a painting
it is of you
acting in *Hamlet*
title rôle, dressed in black
but you cannot hold still
relentless hands roll your own
grip endless cold milky teas

the pose enters everyday life
you go to work, take classes
in booklined rooms teach poetry
stride the length of lecture theatres
hair swept across brow

as Ophelia it's all I can do
not to strew weeds in your path
the time of my playing
sweet to your virility
has passed, so brief
your eye on a future
me offstage somewhere, drowning
you plotting the next scene
a leap into the gaping earth
fitting end to strut, proclaim

but I bypass that river
write out the funeral
take up brush instead
set to on this belated canvas
painting life into art

Late Summer, Largs Bay

By the pier on pitted sand
I kick off shoes, hitch knickers
into sheer cotton shift

marvel at spread of sun
a caramelised orange
prepare for its plunge
into toffee sauce sea

beachgoers pause
as seagulls chorus
the slipping light

above, the flat white dish
serves itself
cools water, silvers shadows

from dusk's pink and blue
clouds merge mauve-grey
this day's divine dessert

and to northern gulf sleeping grounds
birds begin their evening journey.

Kite Flying, Semaphore

At a roaring distance
you fix strings

we stoop to children
guide small fingers

into plastic rings
yell, 'Hold hard'

then kites rise
like dune flowers

over whip of sand
in a high spring wind.

When we command
'Make sure not to let go'

all but the last words are lost
and the kites soar free.

You chase the coloured silks
further down the shore

and the long, low surf
rumbles its farewell.

Central Market, May

Through the chill lanes of stalls
stacked early with fresh produce

peas, beets and first mandarins
Spanish music ignites the shoppers

wild precision of sound and step
the circling couple a whirl

staccato clapped hands
stamped feet Flamenco

aubergine-satined and lemon-frilled
spinning to riotous applause

the Saturday morning crowd
from their frigid start thawed

to load baskets with flowers
bunches of herbs, or pull

from a favourite stall, the last
long loaf of bread before lunch

to head home with gypsy music
ringing warm through their skins.

Adelaide Girls High School

Over the wall the old place
state's earliest for girls
abandoned, boarded and razor-wired
with the sign: No Entry.
Burnt, unsafe Gothic arches
desolate grounds and emptied pool
are visible only from bus window
as passengers alight …

and I am there, 1972
bikini-clad, shivering
by cold iron shed
sneaking glances sideways —
at recess we leant over
bluestone and redbrick fence
to talk to boys
to grate against our fortification.

Now from outside looking in
ghosts run a chiaroscuro
black blazers, berets, box pleats
(and, according to rule, black bloomers)
cross-hatched on tarmac yards
from a fretwork of belonging
an architecture of place.

Return

Central Market

With short swing skirt of viridian
matching crop jacket
all underlined with cobalt
tights and skivvy

the dangling baubles
from each ear look Greek

hand-painted ancient pattern
beads hawked each day
at the Plaka or island market
to new world travellers
anxious for trinkets of old culture

perhaps she's just returned
from an Aegean foray
now fills her backpack
with this week's fresh produce

slender celery replacing
soiled socks, sweaty singlets
or the rugged twill shorts
common to the young

now shopping the familiar horizon
made new.

Physics

I
People like to keep doing
what they're doing
                      — we are all
inherently lazy.

You were
mornings sleeping in
till shoved out
clocking off work
when the hands met
home always in time
for dinner.

It was the sort of stuff
one doesn't push around
                        not easily.

Such a mass
you required
more force
than I could muster

I remained inert.

II
So why does the apple fall?

We are attracted
some time or later
to objects beyond
our control.

I felt the crack
on my skull, splitting
blowing apart
each atom of our
quotidian life.
I had to run
for cover.

Each of us is
inexorably pulled
down

all works towards chaos
disintegration.

Melrose Monument

Glinting in the sun's last
glance at Mt. Remarkable
the plane's debris

a terrain so difficult
rescuers left twisted metal

all they could do
was retrieve the bodies

Mid-North family
flying light aircraft
home for Christmas

losing sight in fog
red earth rising
herald of the Flinders Ranges

and deep in the bush crevice
the crash site twinkles

like candles lit
in remembrance.

Our old miner's cottage

is a house full of ghosts
we heard from the neighbours
how she'd despaired of her husband
him off down the pub each night
and she said she'd do herself in
if he didn't stop.

So that windy night
when verandah slats rattled,
the reek of copper
a taste across the arid land,
he finally made his way home
to find her swinging in the dark air.

My sister-in-law claims to have woken
after a nap in the back room
spied her, prone on the next bed
seems she'd just roused herself
from a long sleep.

Another cottage I know
has a resident family of spooks
lights go out at odd moments
funny noises echo.
It's said they don't like visitors
that they lay claim to the place.

I remember my brother and me
frightened by a snake
no-one believed us
said we'd dreamt a phantom
but we knew it was chasing us
keeping guard the old bedroom.

He's not here now to verify that story
I saw him last year
after the overdose
laid out on the metal bed
and there really was
no waking up.

After the Funeral

here at the kitchen table
she asks to help with dinner
will make the Greek salad
gathers a tomato, kos, cucumber
'Add the feta with the dressing,' I say
and am ignored
she frowns over the onion
knife, too substantial for her fine hand
skitters across fingers, slices flesh

but it is still the dinosaur bandaid
she chooses to wear
a first ornament for her
evening into womanhood

The end of the drought

Highlands, NSW

brings more rain
than you would imagine

listening in the night
you smell the very hour
the tin roof stills

upon waking
in the early light
you're not surprised
at its leadenness

wet sheets strung low
tank's first overflow

or when coming down
the mountain track
that passes as a road
littered with new rockfall
branches like chewed twigs
flanked by creeks
running faster on the dirt
than you dare drive

onto the valley floor
at the view to the west
of placid cattle grazing
water lapping around their legs

and the farmer in her paddock
rubber boots kicking high
sloshing in the new green.

My face

is burning
as if held too long
under the sun
cheeks glowing embers
eyebrows performing stark dashes
punctuations of malaise
or love, it's like being in love
either for the first, or last time
when you'd forgotten its power
of transformation
tumbling from your very firmness
all sense of proportion
sighs, tears, curling in bed
aquiver for arms to contain you
and dreaming, nights, days
hands always figuring
restless, imperative
pushing hair from dry mouth
wiped hands against damp thighs
words tumbling out
then losing it, falling dumb
as now
where I lie
fever-wracked and smitten
emblazoned by signs and symptoms
this year's best, the flu

Watson on Holmes

it's as if he's been unable to face
this one last case: our own mortality

me, I've been making plans for years
moving furniture
into the comfy room
pruned my needs to the spare
black typewriter, well travelled
one desk, lamp, chair

but he, all the while
has not stirred
ten fingertips splay
one hand to the other
in fastidious prayer
I never could admire
he's ossified
skeleton, ghost, younger self

there are clues for me to order
it will all be a matter of logic:
1. our flesh will decay, our bones crumble
2. in peace I lay me down, but
3. he is transporting himself
        into another realm

Gastric Juice

pumped from my stomach
juice sharp enough
it dissolves gold
houses bugs
crazy for the pH
stripping-car-strength acid
parts set out in the wrecker's yard
millimetre by millimetre
shedding metal skin
like my guts
cell by cell
sloughing off the lining
just as in oysters
where hourly irritation
grain by grain
sand creates pearls
my ulcer, a flaming
jewel of passion

Travelling

within Aegina's harbour
the last of winter
rattled the queued masts

our ferry berthed at the jetty
to a racket of children
only one articulate:

'Lady, here, stay at my aunt's room.
Cheap, clean, a good shower for you'

he did not say cold
nor that the house smelt
                of salt, oil
— shade under the vine

I was fresh and raw
as the tiny island
and could enter the vast blue

sky and wind
blasting across sea-polished stones
rolling under my feet

NIGHT FISHING

by **Jim Puckridge**

I was born in Port Lincoln in 1941. I grew up in what was then a wild and beautiful coastal environment, and with parents who loved the bush, the sea and books. I studied English at Adelaide University and then taught in Australia and overseas. When my marriage broke up, I reviewed my life, gave up teaching and enrolled in a degree in biological science — so returning to my childhood engagement with the natural world. Through most of my life I have written poetry, but the poems in this selection are all recent.

ACKNOWLEDGEMENTS

The poems 'Night Fishing' and 'Garage Dreams' were published in *Friendly Street Reader 24* (2000) pp. 78–79. My contribution to this volume is dedicated to my dear companion, Philippa Kneebone, whose responses to the poems have sharpened their integrity. The poems have also benefited greatly from the encouragement and insight of fellow writers Mike Kokkinn, Jules Koch, Anna Brooks, Jude Aquilina and Charles Clennell.

THE POEMS

Islands

My father told me of the islands
Far south of our calm bay,
Blue as whales and misty,
Foaming through the long swells
That sweep unending round the Pole.

He told me of sharks there
That shouldered his boat
As if the sea had turned in sleep,
And waves that rose on tranquil days
Like sudden cliffs, on hidden reefs.

I saw his islands later,
From high on Cape Catastrophe.
That close they looked less like whales
Than sheep paddocks come adrift,
Humble as Flinder's sailors drowned
Whose plain names they bore:
Williams, Hopkins, Lewis, Smith.

But Thistle, the leviathan,
With ruddy slopes like dragon's flanks,
And Wedge and Neptunes further south
Poised to sound below the verge,
These could not be captured, tethered,
Towed home and rendered down.

My father's dead. I'm fifty-six
And still no closer to his shores,
Content to let his islands swim
Oceans of the marvellous.

Outback

Perched on the sofabed
Watching Ti Kanowa's
Outback opera,
I fork rice and fish
From a bowl in my lap.

Those bare, splendid shoulders
Launch a voice that levels
My sleepout walls,
Opens enormous space —
My uggboots dangle in the dark,
I cry into my ginger fish
From pity and a strange relief
To find the universe so large,
Me so small.

Time Travel

On Sunday nights, us kids
Would play for ages in the bath —
Chipheater roaring,
Dew on corrugated walls,
Concrete floor awash
And clots of suds flying.

Bullies, deaths of cats, parental wars,
Being shut outside, existed only
Like the night and rain,
To charge with danger our delight.

Like Tardis, our cosy shed
Roars forever through the dark,
Escaping yesterday's grazed knees
And school tomorrow.

To Bed 1

I am first beneath the quilt.
You strip and toss your clothes,
Stand astride before the mirror,
Brush back hard your hair.

Years of nights
I've watched you,
Draw down that black mane
From brow to shoulder.

I know the fabric of your voice
And creamy sliding of your skin.
I don't know what you see
Dreaming beyond the glass,
Or how your feet feel
Braced upon this floor.

I only know you will
And will not come to bed.

Roads

When you drive on dirt roads,
Drift along laterite gravels,
Drag and slew in sandy wallows,
Skip holes, skirt rocks,
Speed to tune the corrugations,
Syncopate on bared roots,

You wind in the skeins of country,
Ochre, white, russet, grey,
Sprinkled with leaves, splattered with shadows,
Knotted with rocks, snarled with twigs,
Silky with polished clay,
Hazy with sunlit dust.

And let country handle you —
Articulate wrist and shoulder,
Resonate in thigh and buttock,
Massage palms with stone and pebble,
Knead in you its grain and contour,
Cradle you through hill and hollow,
Sway to sleep, as evening comes,
Your urban craving to arrive.

Ocean House

Sometimes when you sleep,
I cannot hear you breathe
Above the wind and sea
And gusting of my blood,
And wait in sweat for silence.

Sometimes when you sleep
I hear the song of galaxies of cells
In your slow breath,
And see the noctilucae of the midnight sea
Glow and subside.

If we could float on this slow wave
Then whales would shoulder us
And plankton browse beneath our bed,
And we could watch the lives of suns
Wink out like birthday candles
On this breath.

Shoreline

This morning, after gales,
The ocean is calm.
A dolphin and calf
Sew the sea's hem
Gently, in synchrony,
Leaving smooth pleats.
Along the beach beside
A woman and child
Pace them, strolling.

To Bed 2

You lie by me, on your side,
Limbs folded each to each
A flower closed.
My hand resting at your waist
Without moving knows well
The smooth rise of your hip,
The smooth rise of your breast.

The wonder is that nightly
You come to this bed
Where all your wit and passion
That flares in the world
Breathes beneath my hand.

Shearwaters

After you left,
The Autumn storms began.
They go on, day after day,
Driving seas heavy as cattle.

Sweeping south against the herd,
Shearwaters fling from wave to wave
Their crescent dance,
Carving on cliffs of wind
Their ancient, intricate pathways to the sun.
The trampled ones arrive ashore
Tumbled in kelp.

Some Mornings

Some mornings, as a child,
I woke and saw
The harbour laid calm,
Houses gathered to the shore
And washed clean as limpets.
On the sea's rim,
Islands bent their heads and browsed.
The sky above, around, behind
Was flawless,
And my throat filled with cries
Wild as a tern's.

De Mole Cliffs

On that clifftop in the sun,
Borne up with eagles
On a crest of stone
Above the hollow sea,
And all the islands
Porpoising afar
To the sky's edge,
Our skins tingling with the sweat
And scratches of our struggle
Up the tangled gullies
To this place above
The thickets of our lives,
We sat on rocks, eyes
Brimming light, and shared
Apples and water.

Kestrel

Our local kestrel
In a gusting wind
Swoops, soars, alights on
A pinnacle of air,
And quivering her wings,
Holds, holds that station
Like a brooch on blue.

Redgum

The redgum by the station
Fountains leaves skyward,
Its limbs gleam like waterspouts,
Its plumes toss on pulses
Of sap from the earth.
Lorikeets in its spray
Squeal like summer children
Hosed on the lawn.

Garden

I stand in the garden
Knowing the train waits,
The Project, the Milestones,
The Workshop, the Launch.

I stand in the garden
Off the rails,
Responding only
To sunlight and shadow,
Sea breeze and rain.

Fungi

In winter, when the streams
Pour full through the bracken
This sugargum forest
Bears strange fruit.

Their life is in the wet dark,
They feed on juices of decay,
But in this undersea season
As winds surfs the reefs of trees
And light is wavering and dim
The fungi like corals
Ripen and spawn.

In Early Hours

In early hours I can't sleep.
I leave our bed and safety
Of your steady breath.

In the sleepout
The quilt is cold.
The moon stares
Through many windows.
Twigs fret against the glass.

My skull is windowed
Like this room.
Night comes in.
My body is a dry leaf
Moonlight will float away.

Shearwaters 2

Skiing this avalanche of air
And ocean smoking with hurled rain
The shearwaters come,
Flint sharp and light as leaves,
Stroking with tilted wings
The shaking bellies of the waves,
Swinging high rebounding from
Their mothering and drowning sea
Then stooping back to touch her
On they dance their blessing of this day,
And will dance I hope
Across all gales of change.

Morning Train

We're carried rocking,
Suspended, dreaming,
To impending day,
Our blood sounding the engine's song,
Our hearts compliant, counting
The wheels milling time.

Gale Warning

The dog and I walk
Into evening, over dunes,
Under muscular cloud,
Whose tendons reaching from the west
And looming shoulders, crush the sun,
Its juices staining this last light.
The north wind, panting,
Warm, waiting,
Stirs the hackles of the sea.

The dog and I go quietly,
Leaving meek prints.

Anniversary

Still warm and halfawake
You straddle me,
Settle like a sleepy chook and doze.
I bear you up,
My saucer to your cup.

Sometimes we swap
And you bear me,
A gull on your slow sea.

Evenings you bustle in,
Exclaiming from the door,
Dump your bags and hug me.
My nose knows your hair.

We fill our glasses,
You unwrap
Cameos of people's lives.
I bring sea stories,
Bird and garden happenings.

In bed you read,
I cup you round.
Then I read and you cup me,
The circle once more found.

Jessie 1

I show my mother
Photos of us kids.
She doesn't know us,
Sees instead
Dogs in trees, an owl,
A sheep with giant horns.

She wants to waltz
'A big strong man
Would keep me on my feet'
And play Australian Rules
'I'd love to kick' —
And spurns her walking frame.
She sings — an eighty-year-old voice —
'But practice gets it back.'

She's not the mother
I recall — dutiful, demure.
She never sang,
I never saw her dance,
And footballers were thugs.

Is this dementia
Or persona long concealed,
Hinted in the grin perhaps
And tilted hip
Of that young flapper —
Sydney, 1930 —
Behind her mother's chair?

Jessie 2

Mother, swaddled in her quilts,
In the armchair at the window
Looks to the sea.

'It's calm today' I say.
'Ashamed' she says,
'Of making such a fuss'.
'It was rough yesterday' I say.
'There is a bird' she says 'So big!'
I see the plodding waves and empty sky.

Jessie 3

I lift my mother from the bath,
Skin damp, hands claws
Legs stark white
Groping the floor.

I seat her, shaking,
Towel her bony back
Her belly and the breasts I sucked.

And when I tuck her into bed —
She snuggles in, a grey-haired waif —
Something is complete.

Jessie 4

Jessie, as my young mother,
Loved the track among the hills,
Summer smell of mallee,
Cliffs above gulfs of air,
And far on the ocean
Footfalls of light.

In dementia, Jessie feared
Trees swarming at the car,
Hills crowding the sun,
Cliffs teetering above
The slow, coiling sea.

Later, in the nursing home,
I think she saw
Chaos outside,
Yet tapped against the window
Hour after hour.

A month before she died
We sat quiet by the shore.
The ocean was still.
Finally she said
'Is this all there is?'

'I don't know' I answered.
She had fought through dementia
To this pitiless, clear space.
We sat in it together.
Round us great winds turned.

Garage Dreams

Dad in my dreams
Your hands delve still
In the Wolseley's engine
Late in the night,
Your grimed fingers lit
By the wire-caged globe
Hung by your cheek.
I lean to your smells of oil,
Petrol and brandy breath.

Your fingers track
Through wires and chambers
Leap of spark, spout of fuel,
Muffled roar of pent flame.
Your silver spanners
Tighten rhythm,
Time the piston's richochet,
Tune the whirl and clash of parts
To a sweet chord.

After, your hands leave
Smears in the washbasin
I wipe away.
In the lounge they cradle
Nape of the violin,
Grip the unruly notes,
Stroke at their fingers' ends
The bow across the fiddle's breast,
Soothe the old rackety
Engine of the heart.

Night Fishing

A boy, I rode nightly
The town jetty's bow,
Heading its long hull
Into the dark,
The waves passing on starlit paths
Murmuring around the piles
In known voices, unknown tongues.

My line felt tides,
Crabs tinkering,
Nudges of bodies passing,
Or something reaching up the line
To grab, tug and drag me down
Then snap the line and leave me
Dangling and dry.

Nights I steered
Port Lincoln jetty
Into new seas,
My line sounding deeps and shoals,
Fashioning at my finger's ends
Monsters and miracles.

TRIANGULAR LIGHT

by Melanie Duckworth

Melanie Duckworth was born in England,
in 1979, but has lived most of her life in
Adelaide, and went through high school in
Mt Gambier. She completed an Honours
degree in English and European Studies at
Adelaide University in 2000. She has since
worked as an English Tutor, Fruit-picker and
Home Support Worker, in between reading
and writing fairytales and walking in the
Adelaide Hills.

ACKNOWLEDGMENTS

Poems in this collection – some in slightly
altered form – have appeared in *dB Magazine*;
Centoria; *Come Down the Lane with Me*;
Four W; *Friendly St Reader 23*; *Gathering
Force*; *Hobo*; *Infolkus*; *Inscape*; *Poetrix*;
The Penola Review; *Spindrift*; *Vintage 97/98*
and *Youth Express*.

Many of these poems were written or revised
with the assistance of a South Australian
Youth Arts Board Grant in 1999, and the
Independent Arts Foundation Literary
Scholarship in 1998.

I want to thank Aidan Coleman, for
encouraging me and helping me to edit
and collate the poems, and my Mum,
Robyn Duckworth, for seeing and loving
the place from which they come.

With You is the fountain of life;
In Your light we see light.
(Psalm 36:9)

THE POEMS

Poem

I wanted a cat
to sit
serenely, with the moon
in green eyes,
watching me
write poetry.

This cat gets bored.

He nudges my pen,
bites my fingers, sits
on my page.
'Am I not poetry?'
he asks,
'am I not enough?'
His purr falls like sand
into the cogs of my thoughts.

And before I answer
he leaps
and leaves,
perfectly —
an Egyptian god,
a fish, a breath
of silver air —
more complete
than words.

During a Biology Exam

Time is precious here.
I feel it rubbing against my skin,
fat, golden droplets,
fructose rich.
Illuminated percent signs
hover,
glowing with potential.
It flows
above the abyss
of heavy minds,
of grey words,
and urgency and
blankness.
It nudges in my ear.
I taste honey
and forever,
and imaginary wings.
Because I am writing poetry.

Letter

There is a smile
in your voice
even when you read.
It dips
and curls,
little waves
laughing,
breaking.

My voice
has holes,
splinters.
It wavers
stuck
in my throat
while my lips
chase
after words.

Tapestries

A princess in a castle
and a traveller passing through
with quick fingers, singing
distant places.
She sits at his feet
(chided by father and courtsmen)
and tries to catch his changing smile
to hold near her when he leaves.
She sees him cold
in dark places by still lakes
and wants to bind the dragon claws
on night mountains
to step behind him lest he fall.
She weaves in her tower
tapestries of golden thread to heap
into his arms at his return.
He is startled by the gift,
wonders what her young hands
have sought to bind in cloth, and asks
what she wants of him.
The moon, a phial of dragon fire,
your kiss, she thinks but only says
'It's lonely here, and I see the same
aloneness in your face
behind your songs, your fingers
and your laughing eyes.'
'I have other girls to sing to
and mountains I must climb'

he says, but takes a piece of golden thread
and bows and smiles.
In her mind it glows
the dark caves and the nights.
But he's seen the places she has spun —
the glittery forests, and beasts
with eyes like the moon, and knows
she travels just as far.

Clasped Hands

(perhaps love)

We are like —
you and I,

they whisper soundlessly
in quiet communion.

Gloves of flesh,
little tendons,
bones we share,
mirrored left
and right
near perfect copies.

Jets of warmth
lace lightening through
twin barriers of skin.

Your cells echo mine
the same swift blood
feeds these fingers
and these
we are two
(though one)
am I am you.

Flesh speaks
seeking silent comfort
curbing loneliness.

Triangular Light

My cat would sit
in a square of sun
if there was one.
In this house
there's triangles
and pentagons
and squashed,
diagonal rectangles.
The windows twist,
flirt with light —
splashing,
mashing alien forms
breathing white shapes
on green carpet.
So my cat sits
in the corner
of a misshapen triangle.
And the triangular light
flashes his gold bell,
splinters
the jigsaw shadows.

Last Night's Dreams

The dregs of last night's dreams
linger, staining my pillow.
I breath their incense
like old wine, and they slip
through my body and the air
where I cannot reach them.
Slowly, like a foetus
or a drunk, tired man
I succumb to their wanderings.
The air and my body fuse
and last night's dreams
like seeds in the sleep-ploughed
furrows of my mind
take root.

(early) Autumn

It happened today
two years ago.
He fell
like a red leaf
tied to a string.
On purpose.

(late) Autumn

The memory flares
briefly.
Fading
like that strange
cold boy
we never knew.

The Second Day of Summer

The sea should be grey
like the swollen sky,
like the wind that fights hair
and crunches paper,
like the cold
still biting our skin.
But despite yesterday,
it glistens —
definitely turquoise,
postcard blue.

In Biology

You traced them in your mind
they swelled round, bulbous,
grapes and honey and light they were,

delicate worlds of fronds, membranes,
invisible stars. You echoed names
repeating softly life's language —

adenine triphosphate,
mitochondria, golgi bodies,
nucleoli, you dreamed

the fluid precision of *chromatin*
and you laughed you thought
they were perfect.

And when we told you
it happened again, you saw
cells bruised, crushed, broken

like his neck,

spilled and dark like
his night and your own and you tried
to banish them from your mind.

But they formed and turned,
fragile, breakable, tumbling still
in curious harmony

like so many moons.

To the City Watchers

You clear away the dust
of last night's snow,
so traffic flows
these early morning streets.
But today, the storm has got you beat —
now out there nothing moves,
save wrens and yellow coated workers —
we stay where its warm.
The power lines won't
thread back over night
to heal this winter-broken city.
Tomorrow, soon
you'll get it right, but now
another sheet-stilled morning.
Pale sun breathes
through torn dark trees
and heavy snow.
Our city learns to sleep.

stammerer

i know the cruelty of consonants
the sweep deep swish
of sss-ss-sssss, the fish gaping
vowels

     BURST!

       BURST!

i want to float
soft drifting word-sea
slide through meaning
weightless/fluid/bright

     BUT

       Kookaburra laugh
          kcKckkccckkKcckkc
helicopter wings whirring
       shatter air

you guess my words
       steal

     RIP

from my throat

CUT

with clear tongue,
precise mouth, cruel

   my words
   choking, knocking, flapping
   dying moths

   stillborn

Autumn Night

There's nothing kinder
than this fire smell
this glass framed fire heat
it speaks
of hot chocolate,
of books and conversations
and burning legs of jeans.

The cat curls, a melting pool
of fur and sleep as
my mind spreads,
little tendrils tasting
warmth, yellow light, red
coals and the soft glowing
crackling fire voice of home.

Mt Gambier

I have come home.
The lake is still
unreachable blue.
I fill my days with old CDs
words and cups of tea.
I drive my brother
home from school,
through streets familiar
from a thousand passings.
The faces behind curtains
have changed
and the patterns I used
to weave my time
are broken, shaping
other people's lives.

Ducks' Feet

Paddles,
rudders,
little engines.
Black fish,
balloon flesh,
under-water wings.
Not even swans
glide.

An Apology

I am a merchant
selling silks of words —
soft, faded fabric
of other people's lives.
I collect pain,
polish it like raw teeth,
blunt and naked
in the warm metal mouths
of dragons.
My tools are words
that hurt me too.

Clinical Depression

It scribbles my walls.

I open my door and her sadness floods.

She lies on the couch and we watch it
rippling the ceiling.

Her parents carry twin oceans.
They step carefully
balancing closed glass faces.

I escape to morning
wonder it does not spill our street
slow the traffic
still the birds

Rain Prayer

Rain splashes, blesses
this alien garden this

walled green square these
tumbling flowers and pillars

and vines. It plinks splosh-drink
in the fishpond, wet

grey mist turns paving stones
to glass. I will stand,

let wet anoint me
among heavy leaves, let

weightlessness teach me
to float — passive,

tingling, exposed, loved
by the small cold kisses of air.

Waiting

Sitting, half an hour
beyond the passing
elsewhere faces

Restless, waiting
for your quick-flung smile
to shake the edges
of the afternoon

You are more likely
far from here
mind rustling
over supermarket shelves

and me
a tired glow
in some forgotten window

Round Green Bowl

'We can't have them on the sink'
she said
of cold soggy tea-bags
leaving dried brown stains
on its silver surface.

So now
the round green bowl sits
by the kettle —
a tea-bag graveyard.

And wet twisted corpses
trail yellow headstones
from its green mouth —

until she remembers to empty it.

Image

'I am the lake's reflection'
says the curved moon
leaping like a silver fish
in blue late afternoon

Sea Song

Walking by the sea in the strong air
you think of girls who lie pebbling
the small rocks
who wait the echoing nights
by the hard sea's moan.
You've seen them often
at the edges of sleep —
the girls with wind tangling
their hair and their skirts, waiting

not for war or love
or the tall ships battering
their grey stone coasts
or lonely eyed sailors
with gold caskets and cloth
from failing empires, jewels
from mountains beyond the sea.

They burn smoky seaweed
to warm the slow nights
the quick fading footprints in sand.
In your mind they wait
among red anemones with pointed hands,
driftwood shaped like water
and the salt bleached shells
hollowed by fingering waves.

Your songs twist in their ears
slip like pearls from their necks
but they wait to risk drowning,
to grow gills and slip to the old world
far from waves and wind
and sailors and their lonely eyes.

Joseph

I remember when the dreams first came. The fierceness of the gift. Bright and strange in the murmuring of sleep. I carried them around with me for days and they were terrifying. I fought them with blankness but knew them to be true, knew God had spoken, through sheaves of wheat and stars, and the sun and the moon which bowed. I sang with them, shaking, and it seemed they would burst my head as I worked beside my brother's rough hands. And here, in the stink of an Egyptian prison, I wish I had not told them. Not for my brother's anger, or the dirt or these dull chains, but for the bewildered hurt, the loss in my father's eyes before he turned away. But to wish the dreams away is to wish myself away. And they are still with me. Weaving their strange poetry, threading the night with a richer blue.